The Complete
FLY FISHERMAN™

FISHING DRY FLIES

Surface Presentations for Trout in Streams

Introduction by
LEFTY KREH

Credits

DAVID TIESZEN is an avid all-around trout fisherman, former guide and co-author of Fishing Nymphs, Wet Flies & Streamers. *He has fished many streams throughout the western hemisphere.*

JOHN RANDOLPH (left) AND LEFTY KREH are two of the most well known and well respected fly-fishing figures of the day. For many years, both have written and taught extensively about fly fishing.

COWLES
Creative Publishing

President: Iain Macfarlane
Group Director, Book Development: Zoe Graul
Creative Director: Lisa Rosenthal
Senior Managing Editor: Elaine Perry

FISHING DRY FLIES: SURFACE PRESENTATIONS
FOR TROUT IN STREAMS

By: David L. Tieszen
Introduction By: Lefty Kreh

Executive Editor, Outdoor Group: Don Oster
Book Development Leader: David L. Tieszen
Contributing Writers: Dick Sternberg, John van Vliet
Senior Editor: Bryan Trandem
Editorial Consultants: Lefty Kreh, John Randolph
Managing Editor: Denise Bornhausen
Project Manager: Jill Anderson
Associate Creative Director: Bradley Springer
Senior Art Director and Illustrator: David Schelitzche
Desktop Publishing Specialist: Laurie Kristensen
Copy Editor: Janice Cauley
V.P. Photography and Production: Jim Bindas
Photo Studio Services Manager: Marcia Chambers
Photo Services Coordinator: Carol Osterhus
Principal Photographer: Phil Aarrestad
Contributing Photographers: Bill Beatty, Chris Davis, Ted Fauceglia, The Green Agency, Mike Hehner, Dwight R. Kuhn, William Lindner, Jim Schollmeyer, David J. Siegfried, Dale C. Spartas, Neale Streeks
Production Manager: Kim Gerber
Production Staff: Curt Ellering, Laura Hokkanen, Greg Wallace, Kay Wethern

Contributing Manufacturers and Individuals: Action Optics – Christine Gould; Tom Andersen; Dan Bailey's Fly Shop – John Bailey; Charles DeFanti; D. B. Dunn; Amanda F. Dvoroznak; Donald S. Dvoroznak; Keith Dvoroznak; John Edstrom; Philip Hanyok; The Orvis Co. – Paul Ferson, Tim Joseph, Tom Rosenbauer; Ross Reels; Sage Manufacturing Corporation – Marc Bale, Don Green, David T. Low, Jr.; St. Croix Rod Company – Rich Belanger, Jeff Schluter; Ron Sartori; Scott Fly Rod Company – Werner Catsman, Todd Field, Stephen D. Phinny; Simms; Lou Spagnoletti; Rob Sturtz; The Waterworks; 3M/Scientific Anglers – Jim Kenyon

Printed on American paper by: R. R. Donnelley & Sons Co.
02 01 00 99 98 / 1 2 3 4 5

Library of Congress Cataloging-in-Publication Data

Tieszen, David L.
  Fishing dry flies: surface presentations for trout in streams /
by David L. Tieszen.
    p. cm. — (The complete fly fisherman)
  Includes index.
  ISBN 0-86573-074-1 (hardcover)
  1. Trout fishing. 2. Fly fishing. I. Title. II. Series.
SH687.T54   1998
799.1'757--DC21   97-49008

CONTENTS

Introduction

More people fish for trout with a fly rod than for any other type of fish. As more people join the ranks, the trout are fished for more often and they become "educated." Techniques that were successful years ago often fail with these "smart" trout. This problem is further exaggerated because so many trout waters today are restricted to catch-and-return fishing. This means fish are caught more than once and will have learned from the experience.

Today, a successful trout fly fisherman needs a better understanding of trout – where they live, what they eat and what advanced techniques will deceive trout into taking your offering. This book accomplishes the mission with superb photos, illustrations and clearly written prose.

The first chapter, "Understanding Trout & Their Environment," tells you how to read the water, where trout may rest or hide and what they eat. A brief but excellent treatment describing the important foods that trout feed upon will alert you to what patterns to use, and even to what type of water to seek the trout in.

Ask any expert fly fishermen – be they saltwater, lake, steelhead, salmon or trout anglers – to describe the most important aspect of fly fishing, and they'll tell you that presentation is far and away the most critical skill. The second chapter, "Presentation Basics," is vital to becoming a better trout fly fisherman. This chapter begins by describing the right kind of equipment to use when fishing the surface, including the all-important leader. Next, you'll learn the critical skills needed to approach trout without alerting them to your presence. Study this chapter closely and your approaches will improve dramatically.

Once you understand the basics, you'll want to move on to chapter three, "Presentation Techniques." This chapter gets down to the nitty-gritty of exactly how to present the fly under a variety of frequently encountered fishing situations.

Finally, we come to the chapter, "Hooking & Landing Trout." This chapter tells you everything you need to know to hook, land and release trout. We'll even give you tips for photographing your catch in ways that capture all the drama and excitement of the experience.

I am certain all trout fishermen, regardless of their skill level, will profit from this book.

Understanding
Trout & Their
Environment

Reading Water

Finding a promising trout stream is not very difficult. Even the most casual angler knows a trout stream when he sees it. The typical trout stream is cold, clear and clean; its waters flow fast enough to keep the bottom relatively free of silt, but are slow enough to provide quiet areas in which the fish can rest. But simply knowing that a stream holds trout is by no means a guarantee of fly-fishing success. A trout stream is a complex, dynamic environment, with hundreds of different habitat areas that can change their characteristics from week to week. And even in the richest of trout streams, only a small percentage of the waters are likely to hold trout at any given time. The first mark of a skilled trout fisherman is not the quality of his equipment or the depth of his scientific understanding; it is his ability to "read" the waters and understand why trout are likely to lie in particular locations.

Trout Lies

In a moving stream, trout choose their positions, or *lies*, based on how well the waters meet three basic needs. If trout are to survive, the stream must have areas that meet all three of these requirements to some degree. And if a fly fisherman is to succeed and improve, he must learn to identify such waters.

First, trout require areas that shelter them from the draining effects of constant current. Trout can't fight a strong current endlessly, and to conserve energy they frequently position themselves near objects that deflect or diffuse the current. Given the opportunity, trout will always look for a sheltered spot that also offers easy access to any food that drifts by.

Second, stream trout seek lies that offer protection against predators. Unless they are feeding, trout seek out waters that are so inaccessible that animal and human predators can't see or reach them. For this reason, trout are drawn to spots where overhanging branches, logs, undercut banks or other obstructions offer safe cover. Water that is very deep or rough also offers protection from predators.

Last, and most important, trout must have ready access to food. Like most animal species, trout live by a simple formula: the energy derived from their food must be greater than that expended to find and consume it. Trout will voluntarily fight a strong current only if hatching, migrating or drifting insects suddenly offer enough food to justify the extra energy required to feed on them. Similarly, hunger can induce trout to venture out from protected areas during a heavy insect hatch, where they may hold near the surface of a pool or flat, feeding greedily while exposing themselves to overhead predation.

With the trout's essential needs in mind, you are in a position to study the composition of a stream and distinguish between promising trout lies and areas where fishing is likely to be futile.

STUDY THE STREAM

Studying a stream from an elevated vantage point can show you the contour of the streambed and help you identify current patterns and locate boulders, submerged logs, weed patches and other promising trout lies. The best time to study a trout stream is at midday on sunny days. Wearing polarized sunglasses helps remove glare and makes it possible to see into the water. From a high vantage point, you will also be able to spot rising trout and determine whether they are rising randomly or in a predictable pattern. Once you identify the types of water where fish are rising, you can concentrate your efforts in the most promising areas.

Empty Water

In a typical trout stream, a large portion of the waters do not meet one or more of the trout's basic needs, and therefore will have no productive trout lies. It's crucial that you recognize this empty water and waste no time fishing it. Shy away from very shallow waters, as well as areas with very fast flow that provide no shelter from the current. You'll also be wasting your time if you fish areas of the river that are slow and featureless, with a muddy, silty bottom that provides little trout food and offers no protective cover.

TYPES OF EMPTY WATER

SHALLOW RIFFLES may draw trout during the spawn, but are simply not deep enough to hold trout during other times.

FEATURELESS FLATS have no boulders or other obstructions to provide pockets of cover. Trout avoid these areas of smooth, shallow water, where they are easy prey for birds.

STAGNANT POOLS with very smooth, featureless, silty bottoms can be expected to hold many roughfish – but very few trout.

Holding Lies

The most common trout lies are those where the fish can find shelter from current and protection from predators, but which do not offer enough food to sustain the fish. Ideal holding lies can be found wherever the water is more than 3 to 4 feet deep, is sheltered with heavy cover and has obstructions to break the current. Most holding lies will hold a trout or two seeking protection and shelter. These are the areas where you can expect trout to run when they are spooked – or when you hook them.

TYPES OF HOLDING LIES

DEEP HOLES, which appear as dark areas in the stream, offer trout a place to escape the current. The most productive holes will have boulders or logs that provide additional protective cover and improved shelter from the current.

LOGS extending into deep water offer enough security to serve as holding lies for trout. The obstruction offers shelter from the current and protection from above-water predators.

WEED BEDS can serve as holding lies when trout bury themselves in the vegetation. The best weedbeds offer deep water as well as overhead protection. When hooked, many trout will dive into the weeds.

Feeding Lies

To feed, trout seek out lies where they can easily find a food source. The fish often feed on immature subsurface insects drifting along the bottom or swimming toward the surface for emergence. More important for the dry fly fisherman, trout also feed on adult aquatic insects on the surface of the water – dead insects, as well as live adults depositing eggs or resting on the surface film. Some feeding lies provide a source of terrestrials and other non-insect foods.

Stream areas with rocky gravel bottoms offer good feeding lies, because important trout foods, especially larval insects, thrive among rocks and gravel. Sandy or silty bottoms don't harbor much in the way of trout food, so it's generally a waste of time to fish these areas. Because good feeding areas are often in exposed, shallow, fast-water areas, trout venture here only when the food is plentiful enough to justify the energy they spend catching it. In addition, the risk from predators is very real in shallow lies, so trout spook very easily and won't remain there after the food disappears. Fish these areas when you see signs that trout are actively feeding there.

TYPES OF FEEDING LIES

POCKET WATER is found in relatively shallow water with scattered boulders. Though it may appear too shallow, you'll often find feeding trout in the pockets and slots around the boulders.

CURRENT SEAMS occur where stretches of fast water move around slower pools or pockets. Feeding trout often hold in the slower water at the edge of a seam to eat insects that are pushed toward the slower water as they drift by.

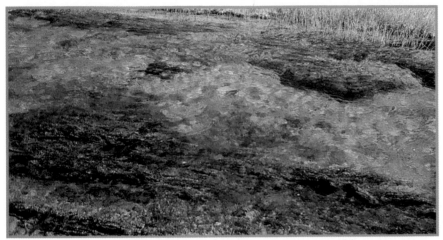

WEED PATCHES can be good trout lies because these areas harbor aquatic insects and crustaceans. Feeding lies in weed patches usually are found near the tops of the weeds, where surface foods are available.

OVERHANGING BRUSH harbors grasshoppers and other terrestrial insects, which often become food for trout waiting in the water below. Brush also provides trout with overhead protection and cooling shade.

RIFFLES draw trout around dusk and dawn, the times when insects usually rise to the surface from the rocks and gravel on the bottom and hatch. Deep riffles may hold some trout at midday, as well.

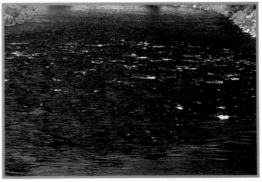

TAILOUTS of pools make ideal feeding lies, because drifting insects are funneled into a narrow area where the trout can feed efficiently while expending little energy.

Prime Lies

The best lies are those areas of the stream where all three needs of trout are met in one location. The largest trout in any stretch of a stream will be found in these prime lies, where the fish find shelter from the current, protection from predators and a constant supply of food. In many instances, a single large trout will nestle into the most advantageous spot in the lie, while several smaller trout settle for less desirable positions. Trout can be quite easy to catch in a prime lie, because they may be actively feeding and not on guard against predators.

TYPES OF PRIME LIES

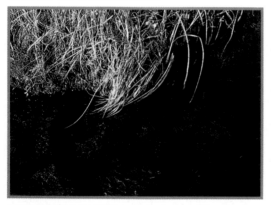

UNDERCUT BANKS provide shade and overhead protection from predators, with overhanging brush and grass that provide food. The current delivers additional food right to the waiting trout. Undercuts can be identified by looking for areas where the current angles toward the bank rather than flowing parallel to it.

DROP-OFFS into deep water, when located near the bank of the river, meet all the needs of trout. When trout are feeding on terrestrial insects in these areas, they are very vulnerable to flies drifted by them.

DEEP RIFFLES rank among the very best prime lies. The depth of the water and surface disturbance protect fish from predators, and the rocky bottom provides a good, constant source of food.

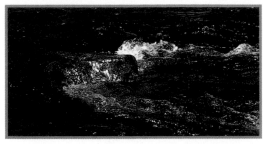

BRUSH PILES *break the current, attract trout foods and offer overhead protection, making them good prime lies for trout.*

BOULDERS *are favored by trout, since the fish can find shade and shelter from the current, yet are able to quickly dart out to grab drifting insects. Boulders and other underwater obstructions can be identified by the boil that forms just downstream, caused by the current deflecting upward. Trout often lie in the eddies that form just downstream – and upstream – of the boulder.*

ROOT BALLS *of fallen trees often have deep scour holes beneath them. In these locations, trout find shelter from swift current, excellent overhead cover and good access to drifting food.*

BRIDGE ABUT-MENTS *can be excellent prime lies and will often hold numbers of trout, as well as sizable fish. Trout will lie in the eddies that form just downstream or in front of the abutment. These eddies offer them shelter from heavy currents, shade and good access to food sources. If the water is deep enough, there will also be suitable protection from overhead predators.*

RIFFLES are characterized by shallow, fast water with a turbulent surface. The bottom usually consists of gravel, rubble or boulders. In big rivers, these areas are called rapids.

RUNS also have a rocky bottom, but they are deeper than riffles, with a surface that is less turbulent. Current speed is moderate to fast.

POOLS are marked by deep, slow-moving water with a relatively calm surface. The bottom consists of silt, sand or small gravel. Shallower pools with slow current and silty bottoms are known as flats.

FAST WATER in a riffle excavates a deeper channel, or run, immediately downstream. As current digs the run deeper, the velocity slows, forming a pool. Because of the slower current, sediment is deposited at the pool's downstream end, raising the streambed and channeling the water into a smaller area. With the flow more constricted, the current speeds up, forming another riffle. The sequence then repeats.

The Mechanics of Moving Water

As every trout fisherman knows, the complex dynamics of moving water can make it difficult to identify good trout lies. To the uninitiated angler, trout behavior sometimes seems illogical. Why, for example, does a trout often lie upstream of a boulder, when the obvious eddy is on the downstream side? And why do trout choose feeding lies on the bottom of the stream when most of the food is drifting on the surface? And why are there sections of a stream where a dry fly drifts upstream and trout face downstream?

A fly fisherman who knows the answers to questions like these will greatly improve his ability to find and catch trout. The first step is to develop a basic understanding of the physical mechanics of moving water – a science known as *stream hydrology*.

RIFFLE-RUN-POOL. In almost all good trout streams, the constant, relatively quick current creates a *riffle-run-pool* pattern that is repeated many times along the course of the stream. The sequence may be subtle in very large streams or in rivers with very slow current, but close inspection usually proves that the pattern is present nonetheless.

Riffles are relatively shallow sections of the stream with fast current. Because of the speed of the water, the bottoms of riffles are generally rocky and free of silt. Since aquatic insects thrive in this environment, riffles are often used as feeding lies by trout, especially during the low-light periods at the beginning and end of the day. During midday, riffles are likely to hold only small trout. However, riffles may be scattered with rocks large enough to create pocket water where sizable fish can find holding lies.

Runs form as the rapid current from riffles deepens the depth of the river channel immediately downstream. Rainbow trout can often be found in these relatively fast waters.

Pools form at the deepest portion of the run, where the velocity of the water slows. Pools often serve as holding lies for trout. Good-sized brown trout are very fond of deep, slow-moving pools.

The riffle-run-pool sequence is in constant change, shifting from year to year, and sometimes season by season. The large pool you fished with amazing success last year may be nowhere in sight this year. As the fast waters in riffles and runs erodes the streambed, the sediments are deposited on the downstream end of slow-moving pools. Gradually, the pools grow narrower, and water is channeled into a smaller area. As the flow becomes restricted, the current again speeds up, forming another riffle and beginning the sequence again. Depending on the nature of the river, the positions of the riffles, runs and pools may change very gradually, or with surprising quickness. During a spring flood, for example, the look of the river can change dramatically in a matter of hours.

HABITAT VARIATIONS. In addition to the basic riffle-run-pool habitats, obstructions in the stream and changes in direction or gradient create other habitat variations that are important to the fly fisherman. These variations, described on the following page, include undercuts, eddies and reverse currents.

BASIC STREAM HYDRAULICS

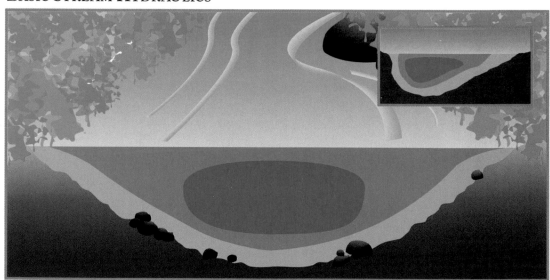

CURRENT SPEED varies within the stream, as shown in this cross section. Water near the bottom (shown as light blue) moves slowly, which explains why trout tend to lie near the bottom when they are not feeding. The fastest water in the stream (dark blue) may be 400% faster than the slow zone. The fast-water zone may occur in any portion of the stream's cross section, depending on the shape of the channel (inset). A zone of moderate current (medium blue) separates the fast zone from the slow zone.

EDDIES *are formed when fast current is deflected into a slower circular pattern due to an obstruction, such as a boulder, bridge piling or island. Although the eddy on the downstream side is the most obvious, the current also slows on the upstream side, which is why trout are frequently found here. Eddies also form above and below points and sharp bends.*

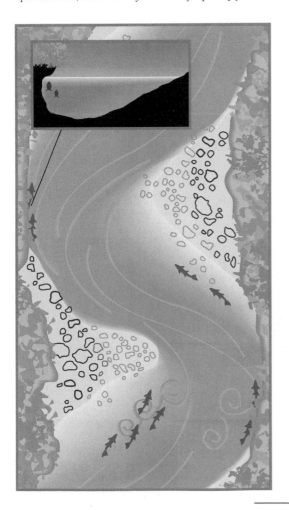

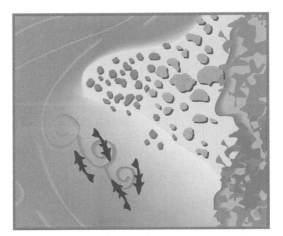

REVERSE CURRENTS *sometimes occur when a pool of slow-flowing water meets a large obstacle, like a point of land or sizable boulder. As the flow is constricted and speeds up to funnel around the obstruction, the slower water is drawn toward the faster current in a circular fashion, and may even flow upstream. Reverse current lies are favored by trout because the current is slow and because food collects there. When fishing these areas, remember that the trout will be facing downstream — into the current flowing in reverse.*

UNDERCUTS *occur whenever a stream meanders and curves. Since the current quickens as it flows around the outside of a bend, it erodes the streambank. At the same time, current on the inside of the bend slackens, deposits sediment and forms a bar or point. The eddies that form below bends and points are favorite holding lies for trout.*

Fish Senses

Experienced fly fishermen know from many long days spent on the water that trout have extremely acute senses. The approach and presentation must be very good if you're to have any chance at catching trout. A presentation marred by a sudden movement, a shadow or glint of light off your equipment, or even a heavy footstep, will send a trout into deep cover. Although it has a keen sense of smell and a well-developed lateral line sense (pp. 22-23), it is the trout's vision that makes it one of the most challenging of all gamefish.

SIGHT. Like other predatory fish, trout rely primarily on their vision to detect danger and find food. Among fishermen, trout have a reputation for possessing extremely acute eyesight, but it has not been established that the trout's vision is more highly developed than that of other species. Its reputation may be due to the simple fact that trout typically live in very clear, shallow water where visibility is excellent.

The trout has a cone-shaped range of vision that is defined by a circular window, called the *Snell circle*, on the surface of the water. The circle's diameter is about twice as wide as the fish is deep. At a depth of 2 feet, for example, the Snell circle is roughly 4 feet in diameter; at 4 feet of depth, the circle of vision is

NARES *are used to smell odors, avoid predators, locate spawning areas and find food.*

EYES *are the trout's primary defense against predators and are also used to locate and catch food.*

THE INNER EAR *detects high-frequency vibrations and helps in maintaining balance.*

about 8 feet in diameter. Outside this cone the fish sees nothing above the water, and the surface from below appears black, or like a mirror.

The trout's field of vision is larger than you would expect, due to the scientific principle of light refraction. The principle states that light rays passing from air to water are bent, or *refracted*, by an amount that depends upon the angle at which the light rays are striking the surface of the water. When fishing for trout, then, you must remember that the trout's periferal vision around the perimeter of the Snell circle extends quite low to the horizon. If you stay very low – less than 10° up from the water at the edge of the fish's window of vision – the trout may not see you at all as you approach and cast your fly. In addition, images on the edge of the Snell circle appear quite distorted because they are severely refracted. By staying low, you improve the chance that the trout won't recognize you as a predator, even if it does detect your shape.

Although the trout's daytime vision is very acute, the story is different at night. Because their night vision is at best only fair, most trout do very little feeding after dark. The exception is large brown trout, which are vulnerable at night to flies that produce noise or vibration.

The trout's eyes are positioned on the side of the head, which gives it a wide field of vision but also creates some blind spots. Trout have both binocular vision and monocular vision. In the horizontal plane, the binocular field in which the fish can focus with both eyes is between 30° and 36° wide, depending on the species. The monocular field, where the fish can see with only one eye, is 150° on both sides of the head, which leaves a

THE LATERAL LINE *detects low-frequency vibrations, helping trout determine the speed, direction and size of predators and prey.*

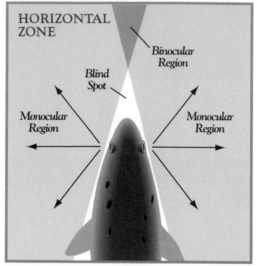

HORIZONTAL ZONE

Binocular Region

Blind Spot

Monocular Region

Monocular Region

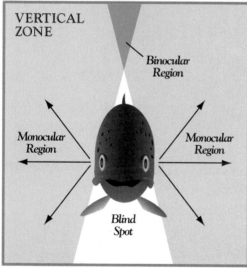

VERTICAL ZONE

Binocular Region

Monocular Region

Monocular Region

Blind Spot

VISION ZONES include narrow areas of binocular vision above and in front of the fish, wide zones of monocular sight to the sides, and blind spots below and behind the fish. Trout usually strike at food that lies in the binocular zone.

blind spot of roughly 30° directly behind the fish.

In the vertical plane, trout have a narrow range of binocular vision above the head, wide ranges of monocular vision to the sides and a significant blind spot below.

As most fly fishermen know, a trout is most likely to spot and strike a fly that appears in its binocular zone above and straight in front, where the fish can best perceive depth and detail. This is also the most efficient feeding zone for the trout, since it can rise to feed and drop back down into its resting position with a minimal expenditure of energy (pp. 26-27). If a fly is spotted to the side in the monocular zone, the trout must spend more energy to reach the target. If it chooses to attack such a target, a trout will almost always line itself up so the fly lies in the binocular field before striking.

Trout have relatively good color perception, especially in shallow, clear water. Like humans, trout see brightness and color by means of tiny receptors, called *rods* and *cones*, in the retinas of the eyes. However, the trout's color perception is greatly affected by the hue of the water and by the color of the above-water background. It's rarely necessary for your imitation to match the exact color of the food it mimics. The general color tone seems to be more important than hue. For example, if trout are actively feeding on light-toned brown insects, they are more likely to respond to a light gray imitation than to a dark brown dry fly.

SMELL. Trout have a very well developed sense of smell, which can detect odors in concentrations of just a few parts per million. Water is drawn into the front opening, or *nare*, passes through the nasal sac inside the snout and is expelled out through the back nare. Smell is used to avoid predators, locate spawning areas and to find food.

Trout sometimes use smell to identify edible food. This ability is often used when trout are feeding underwater on slow-moving targets, but is less important when the fish are feeding on foods that are rapidly moving across the surface of the water. When surface feeding, vision and lateral-line sense enable trout to locate prey almost instantly.

Though the trout's sense of smell is more important when fishing the subsurface, it is still a consideration for the surface angler. Always try to avoid any unnatural odors on your flies and wading gear.

Research has shown that some species of the trout family can sense a chemical called L-serine, which is emitted by bears as well as by humans, and will avoid waters containing this substance.

LATERAL LINE. The lateral-line system is a network of ultrasensitive nerve endings found along the side of the trout's body. The lateral line senses low-frequency vibrations of objects in the water that are near but not touching the fish. This allows it to determine the speed, direction of movement, and size of predators and prey moving through the water. In dirty waters, the lateral line can be even more important than sight when the fish is feeding.

When wading the stream or walking the bank, an experienced fly fisherman steps very carefully to avoid making noises that can spook the fish. Kicking an underwater stone or tromping with heavy footsteps on the adjacent riverbank may be all it takes to scare away or alert every trout in the immediate neighborhood.

HEARING. Fish hear sound with a different sensory system than they use to detect vibrations. Although they don't have external ears – which are not needed because sound travels well through water – trout do have an inner ear that functions much the same way as human ears. Tiny bones and semicircular canals in the inner ear perceive high-frequency vibrations or waves. The inner ear also helps the fish maintain its balance in the current.

Feeding Behavior

Understanding the trout's feeding preferences and habits will make it possible for you to choose the right fly for any situation and present it in a way that gives you an excellent chance at catching fish.

Trout are opportunistic feeders that will feed on nearly any food item that provides adequate nourishment – provided it doesn't require too much energy to catch. When they are young, trout feed primarily on immature aquatic insects and on other small foods, such as scuds. When these foods are abundant, trout may feed on them for their entire lives.

As trout grow larger, however, they often seek larger food items to satisfy their increased energy needs. Mature trout feed regularly on large subsurface foods, such as minnows, crayfish and leeches. They are also more likely to surface-feed on mature insects, which offer more nourishment than tiny larval insects. Presenting flies that imitate adult aquatic insects and terrestrials is the primary focus of the surface fisherman. It's also possible to surface-fish with a frog or mouse imitation, a strategy that often draws violent strikes and some of the most exciting trout fishing you're likely to experience.

To successfully fish the surface, you must always remember the basic rule of trout behavior: the fish simply won't feed on any item that requires excessive energy to catch. In other words, not only must you select a fly that successfully mimics an actual food item, you must also present it in a manner that manages to be both natural and irresistible. If you succeed, however, your catch will be well worth the effort.

When a trout takes a floating insect, the resulting surface disturbance is called a *rise*. Observing a rise can tell you not only where the fish is located, but also what it's eating. Inexperienced fishermen often make the mistake of casting directly to a rise in hopes of catching the trout. But in most cases, the rise occurs well downstream of the trout's lie (opposite). If you cast straight to the rise, your fly will likely fall in the trout's blind spot and will be ignored. In most cases, the best presentation is to deliver the fly slightly upstream of the rise, preferably within the trout's zone of binocular vision.

In very slow currents, however, trout sometimes continue to travel forward rather than return to a holding lie after each rise. When you see a trout behaving this way, try to anticipate where the fish will travel next and cast to that spot. Don't cast too close to the last rise when trout are in this kind of feeding pattern, because you have a good chance of spooking the fish. If you lead the fish too much, on the other hand, you'll usually be able to recast.

Rises can be categorized according to the foods the fish are eating and by the types of water they are feeding in. By carefully observing how trout are rising, you may be able to determine the type of insect being eaten, and maybe even its life stage. This information can help you create a strategy for catching the trout. The photos on pages 28 and 29 show how to identify and interpret some of the most common rise forms.

STAGES OF A TROUT RISE

1 HOLD. *The trout faces into the current when feeding, watching the surface directly ahead to spot insects and other food items drifting into the window of vision.*

2 DRIFT. *After spotting an insect, the trout begins to drift downstream, examining the potential meal while adjusting its fins to rise to the surface. The drift may be very short, or as long as 25 feet, depending on the speed of the current and the nourishment value of the food.*

3 RISE. *The trout disturbs the surface as it takes the insect, creating a splash or dimpling the water with a noticeable ring. If you see bubbles left behind, it's a good indication that the food was taken on the surface rather than just below it – when inhaling a fly on the surface, trout often take in air, which they expel through their gills.*

4 RETURN. *The trout returns upstream to its lie immediately after the rise. The distance between the rise and the lie depends on the water depth and current speed. In waters 3 feet deep or less, a dry fly delivered to a spot 3 to 4 feet up-current from the rise will drift directly over the trout's lie.*

SIPPING RISE. *This type of subtle rise generally indicates that fish are leisurely feeding on flies resting on the surface of the water. As the trout sucks in an insect, it creates a series of concentric rings. Sipping rises are difficult to spot in rough water. Trout feeding in sips are vulnerable to an adult fly imitation cast well ahead of the rise, provided the fly resembles the actual insects being eaten.*

HEAD-AND-TAIL RISE. *This rise usually means the trout is feeding on insects stuck in the surface film. The trout's head appears first; then the dorsal fin and tail are visible as the fish rolls. An angler often gets results by presenting a fly that resembles a terrestrial, an emerging aquatic insect or a spent adult insect. The best presentation is to cast the fly up-current from the trout's last rise and let it drift naturally past the lie.*

SPLASHY RISE. *If the trout completely clears the water or splashes the surface while feeding, it may be taking emerging insects breaking through the surface film or adult insects fluttering across the water to deposit eggs. A splashy rise may also occur in fast water, where a trout has little time to examine the food before taking it. When presenting to trout feeding in this way, you can skitter caddisfly imitations or dead-drift emerger patterns. In fast water, searching or attractor patterns also may draw splashy rises.*

TAILING. *Fishermen often mistake a "tailing" fish for a feeding rise. In all likelihood, these fish are rooting for immature insects or other foods from the bottom of the stream. Trout behaving this way aren't likely to take a dry fly; you should fish using sub-surface techniques instead.*

Surface Foods & Imitations

For a trout angler fishing the surface, the general goal is to present an imitation fly that adequately resembles a type of food the trout expects to find near the surface of the water. The most popular ammunition in the fisherman's arsenal: *dry flies*, which are imitations of adult aquatic insects; *terrestrials*, which imitate insects born on land; and *surface bugs*, which mimic mice and other small animals that trout occasionally feed upon. For this discussion, the term *surface flies* includes all three general types.

Many surface trout anglers place great importance on the ability to choose flies that precisely imitate the foods which trout are feeding on at any given moment. As a result, manufacturers offer a bewildering assortment of flies, designed to exactly mimic all the life phases of any bug that any trout might ever consume. But in reality, such painstaking mental effort on the part of the fly fisherman is rarely necessary and is sometimes even counterproductive. It's true that surface-feeding trout will occasionally hit very specifically on one insect imitation only, but this is the exception rather than the rule.

For most of their lives, trout eat nonselectively, both below the water and on the surface, consuming whatever natural food sources present themselves. Even when trout are feeding selectively at the surface – as sometimes happens when a big insect hatch occurs – it's not always necessary to mimic the natural insects exactly. In many cases, an imitation must simply approximate the shape, size and color of a natural. And sometimes the best fly will be one that looks nothing like any food the trout expects to see. Choosing a fly design is often more a matter of personal preference than of objective science.

SEASONS

Water temperature can also affect feeding activity. In spring, trout are most active in the afternoon when the water is warm. But in late summer, they feed in the early morning when the water is coolest.

At times, however, you'll run across trout that are feeding very specifically on one type of food. For these occasions, it's helpful to have a basic understanding of common trout foods and their life cycles, as described on the following pages. Except for the larger stonefly species, which spend two years as nymphs before hatching, most aquatic insects hatch once each year. Variations in the weather and water levels can cause the exact hatch times to vary, but studying a river will generally tell you the right time to fish a particular fly. Take note of the calendar dates and time of day when you see insect hatches occurring, and file this information away for future reference. Fly-shop owners and other fishermen often can be helpful, and river-specific guidebooks may contain information on typical hatch dates for insects.

GENERAL SURFACE FLY CATEGORIES

Blue-wing Olive

Adams

Royal Wulff

IMITATORS *are tied in such a way as to represent a specific natural insect – either at a mature adult phase or an immature emerger stage of its development.*

SEARCHING PATTERNS *have the general look of a natural, but do not resemble any specific insect.*

ATTRACTORS *are deliberately designed so they don't resemble any natural food. Trout take these flies out of curiosity or defensive fear.*

DRY FLY DESIGN CATEGORIES

Spinner

Upright Wing

Down Wing

Thorax

Parachute

Bivisible

No-hackle

DRY FLIES – *imitations of aquatic insects – can be categorized according to the insect stage being imitated, or by the type of fly design. A spinner, for example, represents a dead mayfly floating on the surface of the water. Design categories include* upright wing, down wing, thorax, parachute, bivisible, *and* no-hackle. *Your choice of fly design is often a matter of personal preference, though there are times when certain designs should be used on a particular river. As a general rule of thumb, smooth, slow waters call for sparsely dressed flies, such as no-hackle or thorax patterns.*

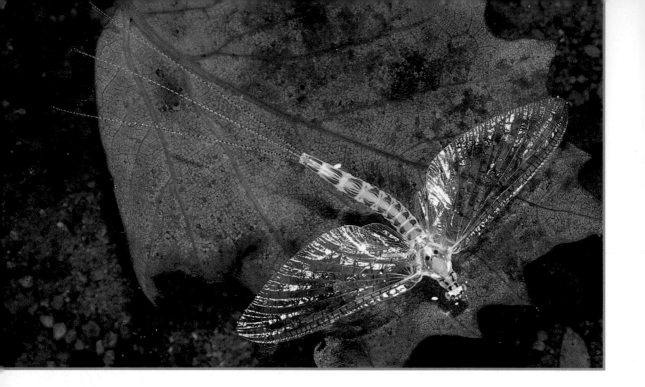

Mayfly (Ephemeroptera) *Life Cycle*

Mayflies are the best known and most often imitated type of trout food among fishermen, and they've drawn the most intense attention of writers. The attention is well deserved, since mayflies are a very important food source for trout.

This insect order includes approximately five hundred species, which vary widely in size and color. Mayflies typically have a one-year life span, most of which is spent in the nymphal stage. When anglers speak of the mayfly *hatch*, they are referring to the emergence of the winged adult from the nymphal insect. Among aquatic insects, mayflies are the only species with a two-stage adult life phase. After developing functional wings, the adult insects molt their skins and transform from duns to spinners.

Mayfly Swimmer Nymph

1 NYMPHS *hatch from mayfly eggs. The nymphal stage can last anywhere from a few months up to two years, but for most species it is about one year long. Four basic types of mayfly nymphs include: swimmer nymphs, crawler nymphs, clinger nymphs and burrowing nymphs. Imitations used by anglers generally range from size 4 to size 18.*

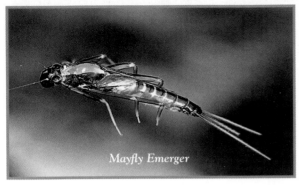
Mayfly Emerger

Goplin Emerger

2 EMERGERS *are similar to the nymphs in size, but appear to have a bubble in the middle of the back, which is created as internal gases build up to expand the wings. After the wings break free, the nymphal skin often remains attached as the adult struggles to emerge. Imitations should be approximately the same color and size as the naturals that the trout are feeding upon.*

March Brown

Mayfly Dun

3 DUNS *have two or three tail filaments, depending on the species. In all species, the dun has two large, upright wings, which are opaque. Some species have a second set of smaller opaque wings. The body color and size can vary widely, depending on the species. Mayflies spend an average of 24 hours in the dun stage before they molt again.*

Mayfly Spinner

Red Quill Spinner

4 SPINNERS, *representing the final life stage of the mayfly, emerge when the duns split their skin. Similar in appearance to the dun, the spinner has two or three tail filaments and two large, upright wings; some species also have a set of smaller wings. Unlike the dun, however, the spinner has transparent wings and its body is usually more brightly colored. After reproduction takes place, both sexes fall or land on the water – a moment known as spinner fall. Imitations should be the same approximate shape, size and color as the dun.*

Stonefly (Plecoptera) Life Cycle

Stonefly species are present in trout streams throughout most of the country, and well-known stonefly hatches, such as the salmonfly hatch of the West, are responsible for peak trout and angler activity on many streams. Stoneflies require cold, clear, unpolluted waters, and because they cannot tolerate pollution or warm water, their presence can be used to judge the relative quality of a trout stream. Because most stonefly species crawl out of the water to emerge, the most important stage for anglers fishing the surface is the winged adult. Stoneflies offer substantial nutrition, and trout often throw caution to the winds when this meaty meal is available. The stonefly species have three life stages: the egg, the nymph and the adult. Most species have a life cycle of between two and four years; most of this time is spent in the nymphal stage.

1 NYMPHS *hatch from eggs. The nymphal stage may last from two to four years, depending on species. The species most important to the fisherman generally range in size from ½ to 1½ inches long, although the salmonflies of the West reach lengths of 2 inches. The color of the nymphs varies from black to a golden yellow depending on the species. Imitations used by anglers range from size 2 to size 16.*

Stonefly Nymph

Stonefly Emerger

2 EMERGERS *either crawl to the streambank or swim to the surface of the water, depending on the species. Most of the larger important species crawl onto rocks, trees or other objects near the edge of the stream to emerge. Swimming varieties emerge at the surface of the water, where trout may feed on them. When the nymphal skin splits and the adult emerges, leaving the skin, or shuck, behind, it pauses briefly to allow its wings and body to dry before seeking cover. Because emergence occurs on land for most species, this stage has limited importance to the fly fisherman.*

Black Stimulator

Stonefly Adult

3 ADULTS *fly or crawl to a land area that offers them protective cover. Adult stoneflies have two tails, long antennae and four wings of equal length that lie flat over the body when at rest. Females deposit their eggs by landing on the surface of the water or flying just above it, at which time they are vulnerable to feeding trout. Adult stoneflies appear in one of two positions on the water's surface. When the stonefly is at rest or dying, its wings are folded flat against the body. When it is laying eggs, or is dislodged from streamside vegetation, its wings flutter. In adults, body colors may be tan, orange, yellow, olive, brown or black; distinguishing these colors is important to the angler choosing an imitation. Imitations range from size 2 to size 14.*

Caddisfly (Trichoptera) Life Cycle

Caddisflies are the most common aquatic insects in most trout streams and are more tolerant of pollution and warm water than other types of insects. Because caddis species are very widespread and can be found on just about any stream where trout are found, it's very important that anglers learn how to imitate them. Caddisflies go through a complete metamorphosis that includes four life stages: egg, larva, pupa and emergent adult. The complete life cycle averages slightly more than one year. The individual species vary greatly in appearance and habits, especially during the larval phase. Since the insect is the most vulnerable as an emerging pupa or egg-laying adult, these phases are especially important to trout and to surface fly fishermen.

1 LARVAE hatch from caddisfly eggs. The small, wormlike larvae lack wing pads and tail, and exist for about one year before entering the pupa stage. There are four basic types of larvae: case-building, free-living, net spinners and tube-makers. Larval caddisflies vary in color from tan to bright green. Imitations range from size 10 to size 16.

Case-building Caddis Larva

Caddis Pupa

Deep Sparkling Pupa

2 PUPAE swim or float to the surface, aided by a gas that fills their outer skin, where they hang in or just below the surface film until they emerge as adults. The body of the pupa may be cream, tan, brown, olive or even orange in color, and there are two antennae swept back along the body. Trout feed heavily both on the rising pupae and emerging adults. Pupae imitations generally range from size 10 to size 16.

Tent-wing Caddis

Caddis Adult

3 ADULT caddisflies quickly emerge after the pupae rise to the surface of the water and split their skins. The mature insects quickly fly away, spending little time on the water, but will return several times to deposit eggs on the surface. Some species swim to the bottom of the stream to deposit eggs. Although they are very good fliers, adult caddisflies are vulnerable to surface-feeding trout. The adult's body is similar in color to the pupa (above). It has four wings that are swept back in a tent shape when at rest, and two long antennae at the front of the head. Imitations range from size 10 to size 18.

Midge (Diptera) *Life Cycle*

Midges include several thousand species of two-winged mosquitolike insects, including the tiniest of all aquatic insects. Midges are the most numerous and widespread insects in most trout waters and are especially abundant in spring creeks, tailwaters and slow-moving vegetated stretches of other streams. Like caddisflies, midges have four life stages: egg, aquatic larva, pupa, then air-breathing adult. Trout may feed heavily on midges in both the larval and pupal stages, as well as on the adult insects. Depending on the species, the life cycle may be as short as a few weeks or as long as one year.

Midge Larva

1 LARVAE emerge from midge eggs. In some species, the larvae cling to vegetation or bottom debris, while in others the larvae are free-swimming. Midge larvae may have many different colors, but all are wormlike in appearance and are thinner than the larvae of caddisflies. Imitations generally range from size 14 to size 24.

2 PUPAE form from the larval insects. Some species form cases during the pupal stage, while others actively move about in the water before maturing. The emerging pupae have noticeable bulges due to the developing wings and legs. Most species rise or swim to the surface to emerge, where they are suspended in or just below the surface film. Emergence into the adult form takes just a few seconds, but the pupae are very vulnerable to trout at this time. Pupae imitations range from size 14 to size 24.

Serendipity

Midge Pupa

3 ADULTS emerge and unfold their wings to dry while sitting on the surface of the water. They are most common in slower-moving water. The adults have two wings, six legs and no tails. Coloration varies widely from species to species. Imitations for individual adults range from size 18 to size 26 for most species. Clusters may form when a group of adults are blown into clumps by the wind. When these clusters are available, trout are more likely to feed on them than on individual insects. Size 16 to size 22 flies are used for most midge cluster imitations.

Midge Adult

Cream Midge

CRANEFLIES are one of the largest midge species. In adult form, the cranefly looks like a large mosquito as it skitters across the water to lay its eggs. Trout feed aggressively on the individual insects. Use imitations from sizes 12 to 16.

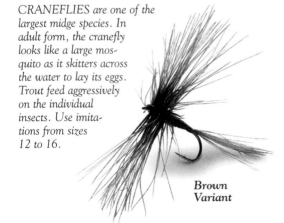

Brown Variant

Cranefly Adult

ANTS are one of the most consistent terrestrial foods for trout – and ant imitations are one of the most productive fly patterns. Ants have three body segments, but imitations tied with either two or three segments are equally effective. Some imitations have wings and are designed to resemble winged ants. Imitations are available in black, cinnamon and varying shades of brown and in sizes ranging from 12 to 22.

Black Fur Ant

Ant

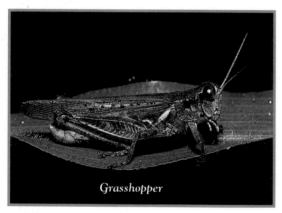

Grasshopper

GRASSHOPPERS will be eaten greedily by trout wherever they are available – most commonly, along grassy streambanks. Grasshopper colors include lime green, yellow, shades of tan and dark brown. Imitations may have wings, and legs that extend through the surface film in the same fashion as do naturals. Imitations typically range in size from 6 to 14.

Rubber Legs Henry's Fork Hopper

Beetle

Black Beetle

BEETLES – both terrestrial and aquatic – are fed upon by trout. Most beetles are tan, yellowish, brown, olive or black. Most are quite small, but some, such as the June bug, provide a very big meal for trout. Beetle imitations generally range in size from 4 to 20.

Cricket

CRICKETS are less plentiful than grasshoppers on most streams, but where available, trout eat them with equal abandon. Crickets have six legs; the two larger rear legs are used for jumping. Imitations are tied with black or brown materials to match the natural. Typical sizes range from 10 to 16.

Dave's Cricket

INCHWORMS are the larval stage of terrestrial insects, such as moths and butterflies. Inchworms feed on leaves and are preyed upon by trout when they fall into the water. Inchworms range in color from bright green to shades of brown. Imitations are typically tied on hooks ranging from 10 to 14 in size.

Inchworm

Inchworm

Leafhopper

JASSIDS, or leafhoppers, are powerful jumpers and are often blown into the water while leaping. Their bodies are elongated but still fairly wide. Although colors vary widely, they are usually imitated with a genuine or artificial jungle cock feather. Size and shape are much more important than color when selecting an imitation. Hook sizes ranging from 16 to 24 are typical.

Jassid

MICE and other small rodents provide one of the largest food sources regularly eaten by trout. Only the biggest trout will take these food items. Use mice patterns with wide-gap hooks in sizes ranging from 2 to 6. When tying your own pattern, use natural deer hair to create an authentic color.

Mouse

Mouserat

Identifying Available Foods

In those instances where trout are feeding selectively on a particular type of insect, one of the greatest challenges for the angler is identifying that food and choosing an imitation to match. During a big hatch, identifying the food is usually quite simple – just look for the insect present in the greatest numbers. At other times, however, it can be painfully difficult to identify which insects are being eaten by trout. In the past, some anglers have gone so far as to pump the stomachs of trout to determine what they are eating, but this practice has fallen out of favor because of the trauma inflicted on the trout.

You can take comfort from the knowledge that it is rarely necessary to "match the hatch" exactly – even when trout are feeding very selectively. Instead, just try to match the general shape, size and color of the predominant insect being eaten by trout.

TIPS FOR IDENTIFYING TROUT FOODS

EXAMINE streamside vegetation. Kick the grass and bushes that border the stream, and watch for any terrestrials or adult aquatic insects that may be present. This method may help you identify food sources that are not immediately obvious.

SEINE the surface of the water using a piece of fine-mesh screen strung between two sticks. Stand downstream from a spot where insects are floating, and gather them into the screen as they drift to your location.

CAPTURE flying insects with a very small butterfly net. Using a net is much easier than capturing flying insects by hand. If you don't have a net available, a cap can also serve this function.

LOOK through binoculars to spot insects floating on the surface of the water. In many cases, you'll be able to identify insects at a substantial distance.

PRESENTATION BASICS

Getting Started

MATCHING THE HATCH?

Much – perhaps too much – has been written about the importance of "matching the hatch": selecting fly patterns that precisely match the natural insects that trout are eating at any particular moment. Identifying food sources and selecting imitations is a subject that can be as complicated as you want to make it – as any number of fly-fishing books have shown. But if you're more interested in catching fish than in identifying every species of insect in the stream, you'll be better off learning the more important aspects of presentation – approaching the fish, casting the pattern and managing the line. To be a top-notch trout fisherman, you don't have to memorize the Latin name of every bug.

In many books on surface fly fishing, the term *presentation* is used to describe the various techniques used to cast dry flies accurately to trout in different fishing scenarios. But this limited definition ignores many important considerations that are just as crucial to successful surface fishing. Good casting techniques and line management are important aspects of presentation, but only in the hands of a competent angler who understands the entire process of presentation. In this book, the term *presentation* includes not only the cast and line handling, but all the preliminary steps leading up to the delivery of the pattern to the trout.

For our purposes, then, you could say that presentation really begins with developing an understanding of trout, their environment and their feeding habits – subjects that are covered in the first section of this book. Next, a good presentation requires that you know how to choose the right fly rod, fly line and leader. Another critical step in presentation is the approach – moving yourself into a position where you can make an accurate cast without spooking the trout. If you aren't able to get close enough, you have little chance of catching trout, no matter how perfect the rest of your presentation.

This section discusses some of the important preliminary steps in developing a successful presentation: the choice of equipment and the approach. In later sections, you'll learn the techniques for casting and managing line in a variety of fishing situations.

Equipment

The equipment required for fly fishing the surface is in many ways identical to that used for general fly fishing. When fishing the surface, however, it's crucial that you avoid drag on the line (p. 51), which can keep your presentation from looking natural to trout. For this reason, surface fishing with dry flies does require some special considerations.

Leader

One item that is very important to the success of a surface fishing presentation is the leader. To ensure that your flies float without drag and look like natural food, it's crucial that the leader fall to the surface of the water with soft S-curves near the fly to provide slack (left). To do this, the leader must be constructed properly.

The function of the leader is to transfer energy from the fly line to the fly, causing the fly to carry past the rest of the leader before it drops to the water. The term "turn over" is used to describe this motion of the fly moving past the leader at the end of the cast. If a leader is too thick or stiff, it will transfer too much energy to the fly as it turns over. If this happens, the leader will land in a straight line on the water, making a drag-free drift nearly impossible to achieve. On the other hand, if the leader is too thin or limp, it won't

transfer enough energy, and the tippet will collapse on itself in a tangled heap without turning over at all. In addition, the overall length of the leader will affect how it turns over. All other variables being even, a short leader transfers more energy to the fly than a long leader.

Leaders can be built from many different materials, so it's wise to experiment with different brands and compositions. In general, the butt section and the adjoining midsection portion

TIPPET DIAMETER AND FLY SIZE

X-rating	Diameter	Breaking-strength Range*	Fly Size Range
8X	.003"	1.0 - 1.8 lbs.	28 - 20
7X	.004"	1.1 - 2.5	26 - 18
6X	.005"	1.4 - 3.5	22 - 14
5X	.006"	2.4 - 4.8	18 - 10
4X	.007"	3.1 - 6.0	16 - 8
3X	.008"	3.8 - 8.5	14 - 6
2X	.009"	4.5 - 11.5	10 - 4

This chart is based on the actual breaking strengths of the materials used in popular tippet materials. Breaking strength on a given X-rating can vary greatly among manufacturers.

TYPICAL DRY FLY LEADER

Stiff				Soft		
			0X	2X	3X	4X
.017"	.015"	.013"	.011"	.009"	.008"	.007"
10"	20"	20"	20"	12"	18"	22"-28"

MICRO-DRAG

Some dry-fly fisher-men refer to a type of drag called micro-drag – minute movements of the fly imposed by the stream's current. These small move-ments are not easily seen by an angler, but they may be visible to the trout, especially in waters that are very clear and calm. In these conditions, your pre-sentation must be even more precise.

should be built with stiff materials, while the rest of the midsection and the tippet can be made of limper materials. In a typical leader, the butt section will comprise 35 to 45 percent of the overall leader length; the midsection, 40 to 55 percent; and the tippet, 10 to 25 percent.

Although there are many formulas for creating dry fly leaders, the basic leader that most fly fishermen use for surface fishing is based on the George Harvey formula. A leader built with this method will turn a fly over but still land on the water with slack in it. An example of a leader based on this formula is shown above.

If you don't have the time or inclination to tie your own leaders, then you can, of course, buy them premanufactured. Modern manu-factured tapered leaders, ranging from 7½ to 12½ feet in length, usual-ly perform well with most surface flies. Since they have no knots, manufactured leaders won't pick up vegetation as do hand-built lead-ers. If you have trouble getting a manufactured leader to fall to the water properly, you may need to cut off the tippet section and adjust its length. Experiment with the length of the tippet to see how it influences the way the leader lands on the water.

In general, it's best to use a leader with the heaviest tippet appropriate for the conditions and fly you're fishing. A long tippet will allow you to deliver the fly a good distance from the point where the fly line hits the surface of the water and will provide the adequate slack necessary for a drag-free drift. Long tippets are especially helpful on waters with tricky, conflicting currents. And a thick tippet, because it can withstand more pressure, will allow you to land your trout quickly – an important consideration if you plan to release the trout and want to make sure it's healthy.

Your choice of leader and tippet can be affected by the size and shape of your flies, by the stream and weather conditions, and by the behavior of the trout on a particular day. If you are fishing large, air-resistant flies, for example, you'll need a heavier leader and tippet to turn the fly over. Use the tippet chart (opposite) as a guide for selecting a tippet size appropriate for the hook you're casting.

In general, light, thin leaders will be the best option in clean, smooth waters where trout have excellent visibility from under the surface. In other situations, however, you can get by with a short, thick leader. On days when the surface is broken by a stiff wind or dulled by thick cloud cover, you'll be able to fish a heavier leader. And if trout are feeding with indiscriminate abandon, a heavy leader is not likely to spook them.

UNDERSTANDING DRAG

Drag is the force placed on fly lines, leaders and flies when they are pulled across the surface of the water in a direction or speed that is not consistent with the flow of the stream. Typically, drag occurs when a floating fly line or leader has no slack to absorb current differences. When you cast across a stream to slower water near the edge, for example, the faster water in the center of the stream will quickly form a downstream bow in the fly line, causing the dry fly to be towed faster than the water surrounding it. Drag on the line causes an unnatural-looking wake to trail from your leader and fly, which will generally spook nearby trout.

Drag is most troublesome in areas of conflicting or variable current, and is one of the fly fisherman's most troublesome problems. The key to a successful presentation lies largely in your ability to eliminate drag on the dry fly and make it behave like a natural food item. Even though some live insects will skitter across the surface of the water, they rarely leave a visible wake. The wake left by a dragging dry fly, by comparison, is very obvious to trout, and such a presentation will rarely draw a strike.

Drag as a whole can be minimized with proper setup of the leader and by casting in a manner that provides adequate slack for the line and leader. It is virtually impossible to eliminate drag altogether, but it is possible to present the fly so it is drag-free for the short period that it drifts across the fish's feeding zone. If you master this ability, you'll catch your share of trout.

51

Rod, Line & Reel

Selecting a fly rod is mostly a matter of personal preference, so choose one that fits your casting style and feels comfortable to you. For general dry-fly fishing, a light four- or five-weight rod will handle most of your needs. Long rods are sometimes preferred for their line handling capabilities, such as mending (p. 70), but a long rod isn't well suited for casting in a tight space, such as a small brushy stream. Because they give you more leverage, long rods do permit you to cast into the wind. For most anglers, an 8½-foot, five-weight rod makes an excellent all-around dry-fly rod.

FLY LINE. Obviously, you'll be using floating fly lines for surface fly fishing. These lines have a coating that is impregnated with tiny air bubbles, making the line just buoyant enough to float in the surface film of the water. A buildup of dirt or oil on a floating line can affect the line's casting performance and may cause it to sink. For this reason, clean and treat your floating lines regularly with a quality line dressing.

An important consideration when choosing a fly line is the *taper*. For casting surface flies, you can use either a double-taper line, which has a long, centered belly and evenly tapered ends, or a weight-forward line, in which a short belly is positioned near the front of the line. Double-taper lines are the most popular because they cast well at short to medium distances and allow for a delicate presentation. Weight-forward lines work well for casting long distances, but because the weight is concentrated at the front, the line will create more of a surface disturbance as it falls onto the water. A weight-forward line is useful when fishing large, air-resistant flies, such as a big hopper imitation, because it helps turn the fly over as you cast.

The color of a fly line makes little difference in most fishing situations. However, some anglers find a brightly colored line easier to see when casting and managing the line, allowing for more accurate presentations.

REELS. Your choice of a reel for surface fly fishing is largely a matter of personal preference. You should, however, choose a reel that balances with the rod and line size you've chosen. You should also choose a reel with a drag and backing capacity that is appropriate to the size of fish you're likely to encounter. Larger fish call for a reel with better drag and more backing.

Accessories

Among the hundreds of fly-fishing accessories available, some are essential, while many are gimmicks that appeal mostly to gadget fanatics who love to browse through catalogs.

One essential accessory for surface fishing is a proper fly box. Choose a box that holds dry flies without crushing the hackles. A box with compartments is ideal, but overloading it can tangle the flies and crush their hackles. And don't forget to pack fly floatant and desiccant powder. Floatants are available in paste, liquid or spray form; when applied to a fly they help keep the hackles dry and ensure that the fly will float longer. Desiccant powder is a drying agent that helps remove water from a "drowned" surface fly.

FLY-DRYING PATCH

A drying patch that attaches to your fly vest is a very useful accessory. Although lamb's-wool patches are traditional, foam patches are a better choice. With lamb's wool, barbed hooks may become hopelessly tangled, while barbless hooks can easily slip and be lost. With foam patches, the flies are held securely while they dry, but can be easily removed.

Approaching Trout

A successful presentation depends on your ability to plan and execute a careful approach, taking up a position where you can accurately cast a fly to a trout's feeding zone. In a good approach, an angler considers all the senses a trout uses to detect predators. Not only do trout have excellent vision and the advantage of the Snell circle (p. 20), but they can hear and feel your presence if the approach is sloppy. As a general rule, the shallower and clearer the waters, the more careful you must be when approaching. In choppy, murky waters, visibility is poor and trout are less likely to see you or your shadow.

If possible, take the time to plan your route while observing the stream from a high vantage point. Before you begin fishing, equip yourself with dull-colored clothes, vest and hat that match the general tone of the background. A khaki vest will look glaringly out of

place if the riverbanks are covered with deep green vegetation. In very difficult trout streams, some anglers even wear camouflage gear. Also make sure your equipment is neutral in color and has no bright metallic surfaces that will reflect bright light onto the water.

As you begin your approach, adopt the attitude of a stalking hunter in a prairie setting, moving very slowly and taking pains to stay out of sight of your quarry. Hide yourself behind rocks and streamside vegetation, and stay as low as possible. Use shadows to help hide your outline and prevent light from reflecting off your gear and into the water. Trout will be instantly spooked by any movement or suspicious shapes above the water's surface, because many predatory birds and other enemies approach from this direction.

If circumstances allow, try to avoid wading into the water altogether, making your cast from the bank instead. If you do enter the water, lower yourself slowly, and wade in a slow, patient fashion to avoid grinding bottom stones together. Move very gradually to avoid creating wading waves – the small ripples that are pushed out in front of you as you walk through water. Wading waves are most likely to spook trout in smooth, slow waters, or when you are wading downstream. When you are wading upstream or in rough waters, wading waves are less noticeable to trout.

The approach is one of the most important aspects of a proper presentation. If you can't get close to a trout without spooking it, your presentation will have failed before you even cast. It's also important to position yourself so you can land the fish if you do hook it.

WALKING THE BANK

Making a good approach is especially difficult on small trout streams. A safe way to scout such a location is to stay well back from the edge of the bank and use binoculars to spot fish rises or promising lies. In clear, calm waters, you may be able to spot trout in the water.

In many cases, footsteps along a streambank can give away your position to trout, since low-frequency vibrations are easily transferred through the ground and into the water and streambed. Walk the banks using the same care you exercise when wading. Take slow, soft steps and take care not to kick rocks or knock debris into the stream.

When casting to a fish from the bank, try to stay well back from the water's edge if the terrain will allow it. This will reduce the chance that trout will see your movement.

Seeing the Fly

When fishing the surface, it's very important that a trout angler be able to see the fly floating on the surface. First, seeing the fly allows you to detect drag and take steps to correct it. Second, it lets you achieve proper placement with your cast. When casting to rising fish, you must drift the dry fly right into the trout's strike zone; in some cases, missing by more than 1 or 2 inches will ruin your chances for a strike. Finally, seeing your fly allows you to witness the moment the trout strikes. The modern fly rod is made of very sensitive materials, well suited for alerting you to subsurface strikes, but since a surface presentation requires a substantial amount of slack in the fly line and leader, it's almost impossible to detect a strike by feel.

Wearing polarized sunglasses will immediately increase your ability to see your fly. Although most anglers wear sunglasses, believing they help see beneath the surface of the water, polarized lenses also help with surface visibility. By reducing glare, polarized sunglasses make it much easier to pick up a dry fly moving through swirling current. Polarized sunglasses are available in many sizes and styles, including prescription lenses for eyeglass wearers. Side shields or wrap-around glasses keep light from reaching your eyes from the side and can also protect your eyes from errant casts and sharp hooks. Wearing a hat or cap can also reduce glare, provided the underside of the brim is a dark, light-absorbing color.

Fish as close as possible to your fly. Not only will the fly be easier to see, but you'll be able to present it more accurately. On the following page, you will find additional tips to help increase your ability to see dry flies on the water.

POLARIZED LIGHT

In direct sunlight, the light waves vibrate in random directions, some of which are not visible to human eyes. But when sunlight is reflected off a shiny surface, like water, the light waves become polarized so most of them vibrate in the same direction. The glare we see off the water's surface occurs because most of the light waves have been redirected to a visible wave length. Polarized lenses work by absorbing some of the polarized light waves, thereby reducing glare. The next time you look at a shiny surface while wearing polarized sunglasses, tilt your head from side to side and notice how the glare changes appearance as different light waves are absorbed by the lenses.

TIPS FOR SEEING FLIES

ATTACH a very small strike indicator to the leader. Choose an indicator that is just large enough to see at your maximum cast distance, and attach it 2 to 3 feet up from the hook. After casting, watch the indicator instead of the fly, and use whatever casting or line-handling techniques may be necessary to keep drag from pulling on the indicator. This method works well where the water has a broken surface and in streams where fish are not easily spooked. In smooth water or around nervous trout, indicators probably won't be effective.

CHOOSE brightly colored fly lines. Bright colors will allow you to visually follow the line up to the point where it attaches to the leader. Though this doesn't necessarily let you pinpoint the location of the fly, it does help you estimate where the fly is located. Practice this technique at close distances to become familiar with the relationship between the fly and the line. When you see a rise in the general area where your fly should be, set the hook: in many instances, you'll be rewarded with a trout.

USE flies that are easy to see. When practical, select flies that are larger and more bulky (A). Flies such as parachutes (B) have a white tuft of hair that protrudes from the top of the fly, making them more visible. Small, dark insects are very difficult to see, but imitations of these insects can be equipped with parachutes to make them more visible. Flies tied with a fluorescent tuft on top (C) are easier to spot; experiment with colors to find hues that show up best to your eye.

FOLLOW the leader with your eyes, from the fly line to the fly. Often, you'll be able to spot the fly by tracking visually along the leader. To improve visibility, you may want to grease the butt section of your leader so it floats better. If you still can't see the fly, watch the end of the leader; look for sudden downward or sideways motion, and set the hook at this moment. Occasionally, you may be fooled by drag, but often you'll hook a trout.

PRESENTATION TECHNIQUES

General Technique

Once you understand the basics of presentation – equipment, approach, seeing the fly – you're ready to begin mastering the art of actually casting a fly to a trout's feeding zone. Although there are a variety of specialized techniques for casting surface flies in dif-

ferent circumstances, some general methods apply no matter which way the fly is drifted to the trout – upstream, across-stream or downstream. These general principles will be discussed on these pages, while more specialized methods are presented in following sections.

GET CLOSE. It's always best to approach as close as possible without spooking the trout. Control over your cast and management of your line will be easier at close range. Cast no farther than the distance at which you can accurately control your cast and effectively manage the line on the water. If you have the ability to accurately cast 50 feet and are able to achieve a drag-free drift, then approach to this distance. But if your practical limit is 30 feet, then don't try to make your presentation until you have approached to this distance.

ACCURACY is very important when fishing flies on the surface. Practice to improve both distance accuracy and right-left accuracy. Pinpoint casting will keep your flies out of streamside vegetation and is crucial for those occasions when trout refuse to move more than a few inches out of their feeding lanes.

PLAN YOUR CAST. Before casting to a rising trout, take the time to watch how the fish is rising. If the rises follow a rhythmic pattern, you'll want to time your cast so the fly drifts into the feeding zone at the moment the trout is due to rise for another morsel. When determining the moment to begin your cast, consider the time it will take the fly to drift to the feeding zone as well as the time it takes to execute the cast. When trout are feeding in this predictable fashion, they often are so focused on the food drifting their way that they won't even take the time to examine your fly before striking.

When using the basic cast in most situations, your final forward cast should unroll above the water. The leader should straighten out roughly at eye level and fall gently to the surface. Lower the rod tip smoothly toward the surface as the line falls to the water.

In most presentations, the fly should land ahead of, or upcurrent from, the point of the rise. By placing the fly about 2 feet in front of the last rise, you can generally be assured that it will drift through the fish's strike zone. Remember that in smooth or slow water trout take their time studying food offerings before striking. For this reason, your fly will have to be cast farther ahead of the fish, and you'll need to manage your line to create a longer period of drag-free drift. But don't cast too far ahead of the rise, because this increases the chance that conflicting currents will create drag on your fly and ruin the presentation.

KEEP FALSE CASTS TO A MINIMUM. False casts are usually a waste of time and energy. You can false cast in order to aim the fly line for the delivery or to dry a damp surface fly, but remember that the more false casts you make, the greater the chance of spooking the fish, especially if your casts go over the trout rather than to the side. In rough water, you can sometimes false cast without frightening fish, but in smooth water, trout will frequently spot your fly line sailing overhead.

MAKE YOUR FIRST CAST COUNT. The first cast over a trout is the most important one. With each successive cast, you increase the chances of spooking the trout. When casting to a rising trout or to a lie, it's best to err on the short side with your first casts. If your cast is too short, you may be able to recast and and attempt a new drift; but if you cast too long, you may "line" the fish – spook the trout by dropping the fly directly over its head. If you make a poor cast, however, and the fish doesn't go down, go ahead and complete the drift-through, using the proper technique for the situation; then cast again.

If multiple fish are rising, or if you see many possible target lies, always begin with the closest one to avoid spooking more distant fish.

COMPLETE THE DRIFT. Allow the line to drift well away from the fish – 5 or 6 feet below its lie – before you pick up the line and attempt a new cast. There's no way to accurately predict how trout will react to a blown presentation. Some fish will instantly swim away and won't be tempted by any continued efforts on your part. Other fish, however, will hold their positions, but will refuse to feed for a period of time. After resting, these fish often begin to feed again and may respond to a good presentation. If a fish doesn't change its lie after a poor presentation, chances are good you'll get another shot if you're patient.

After a misplaced drift, use care when picking up line off the water for the next backcast. Take every precaution to make your presentation behave the way a natural food item appears to a trout. Any unnatural action will alarm the fish and make it difficult or impossible to catch.

RIPPING line off the water will disturb the water and spook trout, especially in smooth, slow current.

Upstream Techniques

Approaching a trout from the downstream side and casting upstream is commonly considered the best all-round presentation method. Because a trout generally faces into the current while feeding, your approach and cast will take place in the trout's blind zone, where the fish is less likely to spot you. This is not a universal rule, however. A noisy approach or sloppy cast can very easily spook fish no matter where it comes from. And, if a trout is holding in a reverse-current pool, it may actually be facing you as you approach and cast.

An upstream presentation has several inherent problems. When casting straight upstream, for example, the leader inevitably will sail over the trout as you deliver the fly to a spot just upstream of the fish. If your distance judgment is less than perfect, the trout may spot the fly line. And even if your cast is perfect, the tippet will be positioned right in front of the trout's nose as it takes the fly. Many a trout has been lost because its nose bumps the tippet, pushing the fly away from the fish's mouth. These difficulties can be minimized if you direct your cast *up-and-across*. Whenever possible, try to avoid casting directly over a trout. If your upstream cast is directed slightly across the stream's current, the fly line and leader will be out of the feeding lane and will be less likely to frighten the fish.

In some cases, however, a straight upstream presentation is your only option. For example, if you're casting to a very narrow current seam with wildly varying currents on both sides, you have little choice but to cast directly upstream. An up-and-across presentation in this situation would almost certainly result in drag.

LINE MANAGEMENT FOR UPSTREAM PRESENTATIONS

RELEASE small amounts of additional line with each false cast, until you have enough line out to place the fly a couple of feet above the rise. Keep false casts to a minimum and direct them away from the fish.

LOWER the rod tip to the point where the line first contacts the water, then begin stripping in line. This ensures that the tip of the rod won't tow the fly to one side or the other, creating drag. A high rod tip creates excess slack, making a hook set very difficult.

BEGIN stripping in line immediately after the fly hits the water. The goal is to strip fast enough to prevent excess line from gathering at the front of the line, but not so fast that you remove all slack and create drag on the fly.

GATHER the stripped-in line by coiling it in your line hand. Strip in line until the fly is well away from the fish or until the line is at a manageable length to begin the next cast.

Another technique is the upstream *reach cast* (opposite page), which lets you present a fly to an upstream trout with little chance of "lining" the fish. The reach cast places the fly line and most of the leader to the side of fish – not directly overhead. The reach cast is one of the best all-around casts, used either alone or in conjunction with other upstream, cross-stream or downstream presentations. However, because the fly line may fall across areas with different current, it is more likely that drag will occur on the fly.

In situations where many smaller conflicting currents are present within a drift, it is important that your presentation create slack through the entire line. In this way, the current can pull the line in different directions without transferring drag to the fly. One easy-to-master method for increasing the amount of slack in the line is the *tug cast* (opposite). Unlike other slack-line casts, such as the stop-and-drop (p. 71), the tug cast doesn't require that you dip the rod tip near the surface of the water – an action that can instantly cause drag if the current near the tip of the rod is faster than the water on which the rest of the fly line sits.

Casting with upstream techniques can also cause problems when you attempt to set the hook. Because the line will be drifting back toward you, following the stream's primary current direction, it is crucial that you manage the line to take up excess slack as it collects between you and the fly (p. 65). This will allow you to execute a good hook set. One method for setting the hook in this situation is called the *strip strike* (left). This technique removes a great deal of slack from the line as it forms, improving the likelihood that the hook will find its mark when you set it.

THE STRIP STRIKE

HOLD *the fly line under the index finger of your rod hand while managing the excess slack formed as the line drifts downstream toward you. This ensures that the line will be in the proper position for the strike. Strip in line and lift the rod when the trout takes the fly. Hold the line under the index finger of your rod hand as you set the hook. This allows you to grip the line and prevent slack from forming after the hook set.*

THE UPSTREAM REACH CAST

USE false casts to let out the proper amount of line. Make sure you have some slack left in your line hand. Stop the rod at a higher-than-normal angle, and point it to the right or left while the line is still in the air. Allow the slack to slip out through your line hand as the line settles to the water.

POINT the rod at the fly and begin to strip in line as you would with any upstream cast. Timing is crucial. Stripping in too fast puts drag on the fly, while stripping in too slowly allows extra slack to gather near the rod tip, making it difficult to maintain a direct connection when you set the hook.

THE TUG CAST

THROW a slower than normal forward cast and aim it slightly higher than usual. Just as the line straightens out above the water, give the line a tug with your line hand – the amount and speed of the tug will dictate how much slack goes into the fly line.

ALLOW the slack along the entire fly line to settle to the water's surface, then begin to strip in the line, maintaining the proper amount of slack at the rod tip.

Cross-Stream Techniques

Fishing across a stream – at right angles to the predominant current direction – is a challenge for any fly fisherman. In almost every case you'll be coping with currents that vary both in direction and speed. Good cross-stream techniques are especially crucial in a fast stream where fish are holding or rising in the very slow waters adjacent to the bank – a very common situation. In these circumstances, it's often impossible to find a downstream position where you can cast your entire leader and line into the slower current. The only way to achieve a drag-free drift when casting cross-stream is through proper line management.

The *reach cast* (p. 67) is one of the best methods for casting a fly across a stream, because it allows you to position the line either upstream or downstream of the fly, depending on the nature of the current. If you're casting across fast current to an area of slow water, reach toward the upstream direction to ensure that the drifting line doesn't overtake the dry fly too quickly. On the other hand, if you are casting the fly into faster current, you should reach toward the downstream direction so the fly doesn't overtake the line.

The *water mend* (p. 70), used in many presentation methods, is especially helpful when dealing with the varying currents in a cross-stream presentation. A water mend can be

executed in either the upstream or downstream position, and it may be performed more than once in a single drift. In the upstream mend, used when the fly is drifting in an area of slower current, the line is lifted and tossed upstream of the leader and fly. This prevents the faster-moving line from towing the fly and creating drag. In the downstream water mend, which is used when the fly is drifting faster than the line, the fly line is flipped to the downstream side to prevent it from slowing the fly and causing drag. It's crucial that you perform the mend before drag begins; careful observation and timing are important.

An easy way to eliminate drag is to simply lift the fly line off the water when it is drifting over a defined current seam. Since there is no direct contact with the water, the line can't pull on the fly. This technique works only if you can approach very close to the seam and can extend your arm and rod so the fly line doesn't lie across areas with different current speed.

When casting to rising fish in very fast water, the period of drag-free drift will be very short — unless you are able to create slack at the end of the line. The *roll cast mend* (p. 71) is one technique that places a great deal of slack at the end of the fly line, near the leader. The *stop-and-drop* cast (p. 71), sometimes called a *puddle cast*, is another way to create slack at the end of the line. With this technique, the slack occurs because the front end of the line collapses before it reaches the water. The stop-and-drop is one of the few slack-cast methods that allows you to be very accurate with the placement of your fly.

LIFTING LINE OVER A CURRENT SEAM

POSITION yourself as close as possible to the current seam. Place your cast above the rising fish or the suspected lie.

Current

HOLD your fly rod out over the seam. This will prevent conflicting currents from pulling your line and creating drag on the fly. The line should come off the rod tip at a right angle to ensure that the weight of the line doesn't pull the fly.

THE WATER MEND

CAST above the fish so the fly will drift into the trout's strike zone. Leave extra line between your line hand and the reel. Watch the line to determine whether it bows upstream or downstream. If it bows downstream, you will be mending in an upstream direction; if the line bows upstream, you'll be mending in a downstream direction. Make sure to begin your mend **before** the bow exerts drag on the fly.

Current

FLIP the fly line off the water with the rod tip, using a quick, short, semicircular motion. Allow the extra line between your rod hand and the reel to slip through your fingers. This will add the necessary slack to the line, ensuring that the rod doesn't tug on the fly. You can mend the line several times during a single drift, whenever you sense that the bowed line is about to create drag on the fly.

70

THE STOP-AND-DROP CAST

BEGIN a forward cast, aiming higher than you would with a basic overhead cast.

DROP the rod tip to the surface just as the line begins to straighten out on the forward cast. This will create slack that will puddle at the front end of the line.

THE ROLL CAST MEND

CAST the fly across and upcurrent from the trout rise or suspected lie. Allow for a longer drift to ensure that you have the time needed to complete the roll cast.

MAKE a gentle roll cast that repositions the fly line without disturbing the leader or fly. Remember that the roll will be directed wherever the rod tip is pointed. Direct the roll cast into the water instead of completing the roll in the air, as you do with a standard roll cast. Repeat if more slack is needed for a longer drift.

Downstream Techniques

Though it's generally best to avoid casting downstream for trout, sometimes this will be the most effective or practical presentation. In some cases, for example, your only access to a stretch of trout-bearing water may be to approach from the upstream side and cast downstream. A downstream presentation can also make sense in situations where casting is difficult or impossible. For example, delivering a fly to a spot under a low, overhanging bush is virtually impossible unless you drift the fly from the upstream side. A downstream presentation can have other advantages, as well. After a downstream cast, the fly precedes the line during the drift, ensuring that the trout will see the fly before it spots your leader or line. And since the line drifts faster than the fly, drag problems are sometimes reduced – provided the current patterns are relatively simple.

You should recognize, however, that downstream presentations are usually rather difficult. Trout almost always face upcurrent, and to ensure that you remain well outside the trout's viewing window, downstream casts must be considerably longer than upstream casts. Managing the line can also be a frustrating experience, because your fly line will cross more current seams, making it difficult to achieve drag-free drift.

Setting the hook can also be more difficult with a downstream presentation. When a trout faces you, the motion used to set the hook tends to yank the fly away from the fish. For this reason, it's best to set the hook using a sweeping motion to the side, forcing the hook into the side of the fish's mouth. On longer lines, the tension exerted on the line from the water may also help pull the hook into the side of the fish's mouth.

One of the few times that a down-and-across presentation is preferred is while fishing from a drift boat. In fairly uniform currents, the boat tends to drift faster than the fly line and will slowly overtake the fly unless an oarsman works carefully to slow the boat. Quartering your casts downstream at an angle to the boat will provide a longer drift before drag sets in.

SET the hook to the side when fishing downstream techniques.

As with other techniques, a downstream cast must leave enough slack in the line to prevent drag on the fly. One cast that works well is the *wiggle cast* (p. 74), also known as the *S-cast* or *serpentine cast*. The wiggle cast puts enough slack on the water to allow the fly to drift well past the rise before drag sets in.

A very basic method for presenting a fly downstream is the *lift-and-lower* technique (p. 75), which is especially useful in riffles and other rough waters. With the lift-and-lower, first make a forward cast upstream and past your target. Then, lift the rod tip toward you to tug the floating fly back in your direction. When the fly reaches a point just upcurrent from the fish or suspected rise, lower the tip of the rod to allow the fly to drift into the feeding zone. Though simple in principle, the lift-and-lower technique requires practice to master. The timing and speed of the back pull and dropping motion are critical to positioning the fly accurately.

An obvious way to add additional drift length to a downstream presentation is to feed line into the cast by peeling it off the reel and allowing the current to take it downstream (opposite). But make sure the current near the tip of the rod is pulling out the extra line; don't allow current to pull along the entire length of the line, because this creates drag on the fly.

Once the fly and 2 or 3 feet of leader has drifted past the fish, tip the rod to the side nearest you. The current will pull the fly, the remaining leader and the line to the side and away from the trout.

THE WIGGLE CAST

Current

MAKE a standard forward cast, but stop the rod at a point higher than usual, and immediately shake the tip of the rod back and forth.

CONTINUE to shake the rod back and forth as the line unrolls. The wider the arc made with the rod tip, the more slack you will get when the line settles to the water.

FEEDING LINE INTO A CAST

CAST the fly above the fish, using a wiggle cast or another slack-producing cast. Lower the tip of the rod to a point just above the surface of the water, maintaining extra fly line in your line hand. If necessary, pull additional line from the reel before the cast.

WIGGLE the tip of the rod back and forth near the surface of the water after the line has settled on the surface, releasing the extra line in your hand. The surface tension will grip the extra line and form S-curves just past the end of the rod. Don't wiggle so hard that you create drag on the line already lying on the water.

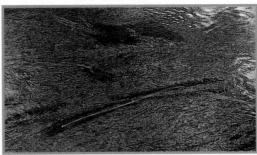

THE LIFT & LOWER TECHNIQUE

AIM your cast past the target spot and upstream from it. After the line is on the water, lift the tip of the rod straight back toward you, so the fly is pulled back in your direction. Don't lift too quickly, or the line will pull the fly under the water. Pull back until the fly is above the stretch of current where the trout is located, then allow it to settle on the water.

LOWER the rod tip smoothly as the fly drifts away from you and toward the rising trout. Lowering the rod too slowly will hold back the fly, creating drag; but lowering it too quickly will cause the line to pile up on the water – also creating drag. To drift a fly toward more distant targets, you can feed additional line into the drift.

Special-Situation Techniques

Most surface fly fishing requires the use of standard dry flies and drag-free presentation techniques, but occasionally you'll run into situations where the basic rules and techniques just don't apply. Instead of dry flies, you may find it necessary to present a terrestrial insect imitation, or even a mouse imitation. In these situations, your presentation must mimic the real-life motion of these foods in the water – which can be anything but drag-free. Trout will quickly notice any action that looks unnatural.

Terrestrials that land in the water generally find themselves there either by mistake or because wind or rain forces them there. When a breeze blows a grasshopper or other terrestrial insect into the water, the insect usually lands with a plop, then struggles for a time as it attempts to get free. Trout are attracted to the initial disturbance and thrashing movement, and if you can mimic this motion with your imitation, you stand a good chance of catching trout.

In streams with large trout capable of taking bulky food items, an imitation mouse can sometimes take trophy-sized fish. Large brown trout, for example, are notorious for feeding on mice that swim across the surface of the water in low-light conditions. Alaskan rainbows

CASTING TERRESTRIALS

OVERPOWER the forward stroke of the cast, transferring the energy through the fly line and straightened leader and onto the fly. Stop the cast with the rod tip pointed at the exact spot you want the fly to land. Don't aim above the target, as you would when casting other dry flies, because the fly will not plop into the water.

will greedily attack a lemming that wanders into a stream. In most surface fishing techniques, anglers strive for a drag-free drift, but when fishing a mouse imitation, a noticeable wake makes your offering look like an authentic swimming rodent.

Aquatic insects, such as caddisflies and egg-laying stoneflies, also skitter across the water at certain times. To imitate this action, you must present your fly so it skims across the surface film. But before attempting this technique, try to determine if the fluttering fly is actually in constant contact with the water, or if it is just flying very close to the surface. If it is flying, you'll be better off presenting a fly with a drag-free drift.

SWIMMING SURFACE FLIES

APPROACH *the rising trout or suspected lie from upstream, and cast down and across, so the fly lands upstream and away from the fish.*

ALLOW *the current to pull the line and fly downstream. In slower water, throw a downstream mend to force the fly to "swim" faster. Mend upstream if you want to slow the fly. Remember to swim the fly directly in front of the fish; trout will be spooked by any action sneaking up behind them.*

KEEP *the rod tip up throughout the drift. Strip in the line with short pulls or wiggle the rod up and down to create additional movements in the fly.*

Blind Fishing

Blind fishing is the practice of working a piece of water with a surface fly when you see no trout rising. Some fishermen enjoy the challenge of fishing in this fashion. Blind fishing may be very productive – provided the conditions are right and you know how to identify promising trout lies. Knowing how to read the water and understanding the trout's environment and behavior (pp. 8-29) will help you understand where to cast when fishing blind. Without this knowledge, you'll be wasting your time.

Blind fishing can be particularly successful and enjoyable when terrestrial insects are present, or in situations where fish are eager to eat any food source that presents itself. In general, waters that are rough and fast with limited visibility offer good opportunities for blind fishing, since trout in these conditions have limited time to inspect an item before striking. Though it's difficult to fish these waters without drag setting in, a lengthy drift is rarely necessary, since trout hit so aggressively.

Riffles and sections of pocket water are good places to blind cast surface flies. Because the flies drift past the trout very quickly, the fish may strike with little hesitation. Searching and attractor patterns (p. 31), such as the Royal Wulff or Adams, are good patterns to use in these waters.

Since terrestrial foods present themselves randomly to trout, the fish are likely to take these insects whenever they become available. Even if you don't see trout actively rising to feed on terrestrials, the sudden appearance of a terrestrial insect – or a shrewdly chosen imitation – may create instant action. To improve your chances, cast to areas where trout might reasonably expect to see terrestrials in good numbers. Undercut banks with overhanging grass, for example, often harbor grasshoppers that fall into the water, so casting a hopper imitation into these waters makes good sense.

When selecting a fly for blind fishing, first consider the time of the year and the food sources available in your area. For example, a hopper pattern is not likely to work in a northern Rocky Mountain stream in March, but may work very well in August. When blind fishing, you should also choose patterns that can be easily seen, since this allows you to see if your casts have covered the lie. In general, large flies are easier to see, as are flies with light-colored wings, such as parachutes, wulffs and any flies with fluorescent wings.

Fishing at night, when you often cannot see your fly at all, represents the purest form of blind fishing. Occasionally you may be able to hear trout rising, but in most cases you'll need to cover the water in an organized fashion to ensure you're fishing over productive waters. Before going out at night, make a daylight scouting tour of the section of stream you'll be fishing. With this daytime image in mind, you'll find it easier to fish productively at night.

When fishing blind, approach the suspected lie with the same care you use when a rising trout is visible. Enter the stream at a spot where trout are unlikely to be holding, approach with stealth, and make your presentation as though casting to a rising fish. If you're fishing a terrestrial pattern, you may want to deliberately create drag to simulate the struggling of a grasshopper or ant. Cast to each spot two or three times, then move on to the next location. Without proof that a trout is present, don't waste your time by casting more than a few times to a single spot.

COVERING WATER WHILE BLIND FISHING

BEGIN by fishing the lies that are closest to you, and work your way out to a reasonable distance – about 30 feet. Casting at distant targets first will likely spook or "line" the fish closest to you. Working the close spots first allows you to catch the nearby fish without spooking more distant fish. After exhausting these lies, move upstream until you are within range of new targets, then work the water again.

HOOKING & LANDING TROUT

Setting the Hook

When a trout attacks your surface fly, it signifies that all the carefully planned aspects of your presentation have come together. This success, however, won't mean much unless you manage to actually hook and land the trout. Curiously, the techniques for setting the hook are neglected by many fly fishermen, who spend hours practicing and reading about casting and fly-tying skills. Unlike other fly-fishing skills, setting the hook is almost impossible to practice without a fish at the far end of your fly line. Accomplished fly fishermen spend a good deal of time envisioning the moment of the strike and imagining how they will move when setting the hook. Some novice anglers dismiss this notion as mental hocus-pocus, but any experienced angler knows the truth: the more imaginary trout you hook and land in your mind, the better your chances of taking actual fish.

A successful hook set begins when you tie your fly, either at home or at the stream's edge. Make sure to use razor-sharp hooks on your flies. A dull hook has a much poorer chance of finding its mark, imbedded in the mouth of trout. It's also crucial that you be able to see your fly (pp. 56-57) in order to get a good hook set. Timing is crucial when setting the hook.

With most surface techniques, you should set the hook as quickly as possible. In fast waters, trout will hit very suddenly and forcefully, and you'll need to set the hook instantly, before the fish realizes it has an imposter in its mouth. Trout can, and will, spit out a fly in a fraction of a second.

The exception to this rule is when you are fishing a surface fly in slow-moving water. In this situation, trout feed in a more leisurely fashion and require a second or two in order to suck in the fly. When fishing slow waters, many anglers miss trout by setting the hook at the first visual sign of surface disturbance. In conventional surface fishing in very slow or still waters, an angler can wait until he feels the weight of the fish before setting the hook, but this won't work with fly gear. When fishing slow waters with fly gear, hesitate for one to two seconds after you see the trout hit. Set the hook too soon, and you'll pull the fly away from the trout; set the hook too late, and the trout may have already spit out your fly.

Setting the hook quickly doesn't mean you should pull on it with great force. In the excitement of hooking a trout, many fishermen set the hook with too much zeal, resulting in broken tippets. One way to avoid this problem is to use the slip strike (right), which allows you to cushion the tippet with the extra fly line held in your line hand. Setting your reel to a very light drag can also keep you from snapping the tippet as you set the hook.

When fishing an upstream presentation, or when you have too much slack line on the water, strip in line with your line hand at the moment you set the hook (p. 66). This removes most of the slack and improves your chances for a good hook set. Make sure to keep the line under the index finger of your rod hand as you set the hook, because this puts you in a good position to play the fish.

THE SLIP STRIKE

HOOK *the line over the index or middle finger of the rod hand. Pinch it between your finger and the cork of the rod handle when presenting the fly.*

SET *the hook with a quick upward motion of the rod tip. As you lift the rod, allow the line to slip between your finger and the handle.*

Playing & Landing Trout

In addition to the satisfaction of executing a successful presentation, the excitement of playing and landing a trout is what it's all about for many fly fishermen. The leaping, the lightning-fast runs and dogged fights are full of excitement and drama – especially for the angler who knows how to play trout correctly. In the hands of a less experienced fisherman, the drama of playing a trout can often lead to humiliation.

Before you head out to the stream, first consider the tippet size you'll be using. Using the heaviest material that is practical will help you land a fish as quickly as possible. This can be an important concern if you plan to release the trout. A fish that fights too long may die from lethal levels of toxic chemicals building up in its blood, so landing your catch quickly has definite advantages. A heavy tippet will also make it possible to firmly lean on a fish and keep it from swimming under a snaggy log or down rapids where you can't go. The only times light tippets are necessary are when fishing in ultra clear and calm waters, over very spooky fish or when using very small flies.

Immediately after setting the hook, clear any excess line that may be off the reel. Once the line is cleared, quickly get the fish "on the reel." If you don't immediately get the trout on the reel, you may find yourself with loose coils of line lying tangled around your feet or equipment, or around bankside brush. If the line should catch on an obstacle while your trout is making a run, the tippet is almost sure to break. Keep pressure on the line while reeling to ensure that it comes in straight and tight (p. 86). This way, if the fish begins to run, the line will come directly off the reel. This is especially important to keep from breaking the tippet when fighting a large fish that takes out a lot of line.

Using reel drag also can be important when fighting trout on very light tippets. On most reels, the drag feature will feed out line more smoothly than you can by letting the line slip through your fingers. With a fish "on the reel," the drag – either a clicker or disc-type – adds cushion to the line and takes pressure off the leader and tippet. Applying pressure with the palm of your line hand on the reel, called *palming*, will add additional drag if needed.

In most situations, you should try to prevent any slack from forming in the line during the fight. More often than not, slack will lead to a sudden, long-distance release of the fish – and instant disappointment for you. The only situation in which you can use slack to your benefit occurs when a trout is swimming downstream toward unchartable territory where you cannot follow. In this situation, quickly strip out line and try to get a portion of the line below the fish. If it feels drag tension coming from downstream, the trout may react by turning and heading back upstream.

Try to keep the fish moving so it eventually tires. When a fish is running in one direction, fight it with pressure applied in the opposite direction, and change the direction of your pressure whenever the trout changes its heading. When a fish runs downstream, it's time to put on your hiking boots, so to speak, and follow it. Large fish use the current to their advantage. They often head to heavy current and allow the water to pull them downstream very quickly. If you don't follow, the trout may spool you, taking your entire line and backing, or it may run into a snag and break you off.

GETTING THE FISH "ON THE REEL"

POSITION the line under the index finger of your rod hand, and squeeze it tightly against the cork of the fly rod grip. If the fish begins to run, give it some line by allowing the line to slip under your finger.

DRAPE the fly line next to the reel over the little finger of your rod hand. As you retrieve line, move your little finger back and forth, using it as a line guide to ensure that the line transfers evenly to the reel. Once the fish is on the reel, you can drop the little finger.

"LINING IN" FISH

PINCH the fly line against the rod with the index finger of your rod hand. This prevents slack from forming as you strip in line.

RELEASE pressure slightly on your index finger, and strip in an arm's length of line. After each pull, apply pressure with your rod-hand index finger as you reach forward with your line hand for the next pull.

PLAYING A LARGE JUMPER

LOWER the rod if you are fighting a large fish that is jumping out of the water. Although a "hot" trout makes for very exciting fishing, the odds tilt in the fish's favor after each spectacular leap. If you keep the rod tip up, the tension will increase and the tippet may break. Point your rod tip at the fish when he jumps, then raise the rod back up in the air to remove slack after he reenters the water.

Using the Stream's Current

APPLY side pressure to force the trout into turning its body sideways against the current. In this way, the fish tires more quickly. As the fish moves back and forth across the stream, change your rod direction to keep the fish fighting against the current.

PLAY the fish from downstream whenever possible. The trout will tire more quickly when struggling upstream against the current.

Tips for Landing Trout

REEL the fish in until the amount of line extending past the tip of the rod is roughly the same length as the rod itself. This will allow you to reach the fish without putting too much pressure on the rod.

NET the fish from the front, where it can swim directly into the net; never stab at the fish or try to net it from behind. Try to draw the fish into calm water, and make sure the net is wet before you attempt to land the fish. Use a net made from fine, soft mesh.

LAND the trout in water at least 6 inches deep, if possible. Avoid beaching the trout, because it may flop around, damaging its protective slime layer and possibly causing internal organ damage.

GRASP the wrist of the trout's tail with one hand and support the fish's weight with the other hand. This technique is especially important with large trout. If the fish struggles free, let it go and fight it back in with the rod.

Releasing Trout

Releasing a trout successfully starts with proper fish handling, beginning at the moment the trout is brought to the net or the hand. If a trout is treated poorly, its chances for survival decrease dramatically. The best way to "handle" a trout is to avoid touching it at all, but when handling is necessary, following a few simple guidelines will reduce the amount of stress put on the fish.

If you can, try to release the fish without touching it with your hands or any other object, and without lifting it from the water. This kind of release is often possible if you use a pair of forceps or one of the specialty hook-removal tools that are available.

If you do use a net, make sure to dip it completely in the water so the mesh is fully wet before the trout enters it; a dry net can damage the fish's slime layer. Don't hoist the fish from the water using the net, because the threads can easily split the trout's fins, especially if the net material is a large mesh. Instead, use the net to simply hold the fish while you remove the hook.

If you must handle a trout with your bare hands, make sure your skin is wet before you touch the fish. Dry skin, like a dry net, can remove the slime layer that protects

the fish from disease. When holding the fish, use a light grip to avoid injuring its internal organs. Holding the fish on its side or upside down may calm the fish, making it easier to safely remove the hook. Work close to the surface of the water when handling fish. A fish held over dry ground, the bottom of a drift boat, or even very shallow water can sustain fatal external or internal damage if it slips from your grasp. For similar reasons, a trout should never be beached if you plan to release it. And a fish you intend to release should never be held by the gills. Many trout handled in this fashion swim away only to die a short time later.

How you unhook a trout is important to its welfare. Try to avoid damaging the fish's mouth. Using barbless hooks, or flattening the barbs on standard hooks, can help minimize injury. If the fish is hooked deep in the throat or in the gills, it's best to cut the line as close as possible to the fly rather than to try to pull out the hook. A trout released with a dry fly imbedded in its throat has a much better chance of sur-vival than one badly injured by an angler wrenching out a deep hook.

Once you free the hook, make sure the trout is in good condition before you release it. An exhausted fish that can't swim may suffocate because it is unable to move fresh water over its gills. By taking the time to revive a tired fish (right), you can greatly increase its chances of survival. Not every fish can be revived, however. An experienced angler faced with a mortally wounded fish will generally keep and use the trout – provided it is a legal catch.

REVIVING TROUT

A fish that is too exhausted to swim or keep itself upright needs special treatment before it is released. Moving the trout back and forth in the current forces water over the gills and can provide enough fresh oxygen to help the fish recover. Holding the mouth open with your fingers allows more fresh oxygenated water to wash over the gills. Once the trout shows strong gill movement and is able to hold itself upright in the water, it can be released.

REVIVING *a rainbow trout.*

Photographing Your Fish

With catch-and-release fishing growing in popularity among anglers, photography has become an important way to ensure that you will remember a particular fish or memorable trip. However, many anglers find it very difficult to take quality photos that do justice to the fish. Some snapshots are too light, others too dark; some are fuzzy and out of focus, others are too cluttered to clearly show your catch.

The first step toward taking better photos is to find yourself a good, reliable camera. For the casual photographer, a good choice is a fully

automatic 35mm pocket camera with a fixed lens. Some of these models are water-resistant or waterproof. If you frequently fish alone, you'll need a camera with a self-timer – and a small tripod – so you can photograph yourself.

If you are seriously interested in photography, you'll want to get a 35mm camera with optional manual modes, as well as automatic operation. A serious photographer also needs a camera that can accept a range of lenses. Mounting your camera with a zoom lens with a focal length of about 28mm to 80mm is an excellent choice. This type of lens allows you to adjust it from wide-angle to low-power telephoto view in an instant, without the inconvenience of carrying extra lenses and changing them constantly.

If you've never operated a 35mm camera, it pays to enroll in a course to learn the principles of photography and photo operation. Short courses are sometimes available at the store where you purchased your camera, or through community education programs. Perhaps the best way to improve your own photography is to study photos you like and figure out why they appeal to you.

The tips on the following pages will help you take better pictures the next time you go fishing. By paying attention to detail and giving up a few minutes of fishing to concentrate on your photography, you'll be able to bring back photos that capture the live excitement of your catch.

SHOOTING POSED PHOTOS

A fly fisherman posed with a beautiful trout can make for a terrific shot – or a terrible one. The next time you snap a photo of a friend holding a trout, pay attention to the following details. The result will be a much better photo.

1. Take the photo moments after the fish is landed. Don't hurt its chances by keeping the fish out of water for too long. If possible, shoot the picture while holding the trout in the water.

2. Choose the background carefully. Sky, water or undeveloped shoreline make good, simple backdrops.

3. Have your friend push back his hat and take off his sunglasses to remove shadows hiding his face.

4. Don't let your model's hands obscure the fish – especially its head.

5. Take photos of normal fish-handling activities to give realism and authenticity to your shots.

PHOTOGRAPHY TIPS

USE FILL-FLASH. When shooting at a backlit subject, you can use "fill-flash" to add light to shadowy areas. This technique is possible only if you own a manual camera, or an automatic camera with an override setting that provides fill-flash. Many fully automatic cameras cannot be set for fill-flash. If you have a manual camera, fill-flash works best if you use a variable-power flash unit. With the camera in manual mode, set your shutter speed to synchronize with the flash – usually ¹⁄₆₀ second. Then, set the aperture (f-stop) on the lens according to the camera's light meter. Adjust your flash unit according to the aperture setting of your camera and the distance to the subject. Finally, turn down the power dial on the flash unit by one f-stop to prevent the flash from "burning out" your subject. Shoot one or two shots; then, for insurance, lower your power setting by one more f-stop and shoot again.

USE LOTS OF FILM. Film is relatively cheap, compared to other fly-fishing accessories, so take lots of photos to ensure that you get at least one good shot. If you like the look of a shot, take extras to compensate for those that may be ruined by movement or an awkward expression. If you have a camera with manual exposure controls, you can bracket your photos by taking shots on both sides of the setting recommended by your camera's light meter. For example, if the meter indicates an f8 exposure aperture, take one photo at this setting, then take a second at f5.6 and a third at f11. This helps guarantee that you get at least one good exposure.

SHOOT EARLY OR LATE IN THE DAY. *Natural light is most attractive in the early morning or late afternoon, when the angle of sunlight is low. Photos taken at these times will have rich, warm colors and uniform tone, while photos taken at midday have deep shadows and harsh, contrasting tones. Midday light can "burn out" details – such as the natural silvery hue of many fish. If you must shoot in bright light, turn the fish slightly to minimize reflection and get the best coloration and detail.*

CATCH THE ACTION. *Action photos offer exciting drama, but they require special techniques. Keep your camera loaded and set for the prevailing light conditions – and keep it close at hand. A wide-angle lens will make it easier to frame both the angler and the fish in your shot. Set the shutter speed at ¹/₅₀₀ second to ensure that the action will be frozen. If using an autofocus camera, make sure to keep the subject in the center of the frame.*

WIDE ANGLES ADD INTEREST. *A short, 24mm or 28mm wide-angle lens makes objects in the foreground appear bigger, while background objects seem smaller. The resulting photo is often more interesting than a similar shot taken with a "normal" 50mm lens. Wide-angle lenses also offer a wider depth-of-field, which means both foreground and background objects will be in clearer focus.*

Index

Italics indicate fly patterns

Cowles Creative Publishing,
Incorporated offers a variety of
how-to-books. For information write:

Cowles Creative Publishing
Subscriber Books
5900 Green Oak Drive
Minnetonka, MN 55343

Photo Credits

*Note: **T**=Top, **C**=Center, **B**=Bottom, **L**=Left, **R**=Right, **I**=Inset*